memoirs from t

– isaac e.j.

First published by Ingram Spark 2022

Copyright © 2022 by isaac e.j.

All rights reserved. No part of this publication may be reproduced, stored or transmitted in any form or by any means, electronic, mechanical, photocopying, recording, scanning, or otherwise without written permission from the publisher. It is illegal to copy this book, post it to a website, or distribute it by any other means without permission.

isaac e.j. asserts the moral right to be identified as the author of this work.

The Fell Types are digitally reproduced by Igino Marini. www.iginomarini.com

Cover art by Jamie Thompson

i.

autumn

BACK TO NATURE

the last time i felt a breeze
was when the final door slammed shut

now — decay is all that breeds
i harbour the memory beneath my gut

in the end, corruption eclipsed you
sublimity swallowed by a shadow
in dreams, submerged in cerulean blue
awake,   the   reality   that   darkens
tomorrow

crush the branches in your throat
where bygone robins used to perch
repurpose our loss as an anecdote;
a   forgotten   punchline   for   which   you
search

> *everything here has been replaced*
> *with manufactured bones*

talk me into a consensus —
     into swapping beliefs like currency;
that these ratchets are unpretentious
     and that armageddon lacks urgency

trade your hearts for metal rods;
to replace the weight of feeling;
to advance despite the odds;
to stare blankly at your ceiling

when your house feels like a prison
it's hard to acknowledge what we won
or ponder the existentialism
     in trying to remember the sun

how i miss the heat
on the nape of my neck
despite the fact i would always return
home
          scorched

             and *sunburned.*

NOSTALGIA

the house still sits –
                    unmoving
each brick and accompanying
slather of cement
perfectly intact

but our fence has been painted over
                    repurposed for someone new
the strokes of intrusive orange and
creme deter me from entry
                    and it's like i can't breathe

fleshy young faces have now matured;
corporate masks clamped on top
growing up served them well
taught them how to find
contentment in disassociation

          and yet it is the shadows
of their younger, livelier selves;
                    eyes pooling with
                    innocence and *familiarity*

that will flicker before my own
          in my final, *bloodiest* moments

for them,
　　　　romanticising moments
　　　　　　　　that have long passed
　　　　　only lures uneasiness
from its locked glass cabinet

i'm sure i was always mildly adequate,
but confession feels like a blade:

　　　　　　is it better to be left to bleed out?
　　　　　　　　or to bite the bullet myself?

this so called natural light
is all artificial now
a mixture of unknown chemicals
　　　　　brewed in the pockets
　　　　　　　　of untrustworthy boys
who say they
　　　　'just want to make you feel good'

and why shouldn't you?
　　　in your gut there are murmurs;
　　　　　whispers that it'll never burn
　　　with such intense laughter again

that the happiest of days have
packed up
and left,

                        clearing a space for
mood swings and tears;
heartbreak and *screaming*;
screaming until your throat burns as
fiercely
as your gut once did

the house still sits –
painted by those
who mirror my
convoluted fantasies
             of simpler times

BETTER ON PAPER

my ink slumped content
      printed;
            centred
in your fresh sheet of parchment
retains the superior sum of poise
to my pitiful twisted tongue—
            watch it helplessly choke
on all the wrong words

my voice,
disharmonious and shrewish
and how i never consider
     the ramifications of my poor choices
i'll proudly produce
every mismatched syllable i can recall
through traitorous lips
soon, i'll escape through
the earthy tunnel at my teeth
but not before juxtaposing
all that sits upon
          dainty, exposed page.

– i have said countless things
i wish that i could take back.

EXPIRATION DATE

i should've known
that this was always
destined to expire

should've felt the ticking time bomb
pressing into my leg;
disguised as some attention seeking
tumour

one-sided adoration clashing with
youthful complexity:
one of us simply brimming with a
naively perceived ecstasy;
ten feet deep and basking in the glory of
our already stitched together future

the other rooted to the marble floor
overlooking the depth and breadth and
confessing in a forbidden tone—
"this will end in flames."

i should've known
that we were plummeting
right from take off:
plain
and awkward
and frankly, quite embarrassing

– the autumn of relationships

co-dependence isn't really your style
but without you,
i'm pretty sure i'd be falling apart
and that scares the hell out of us,
so let's count our palpitations together;
twist the concept into a game–
fits the theme, right?

i thought i was the perfectionist but it
seems you are not willing to even
acknowledge the endless rattling in your
chest; its desperation evoking ignorance
and then acquiescing to sign your soul
away to me after forty five minutes of
agonising silence

like a child chooses
a favourite toy,
            i chose *you*

                    and i spent hours smiling
                            foolishly,
interlocking my own fingers
and thinking of you
        sinking into the paradise
i had visualised
especially for when
            you became mine
                    at long last

impermanence is a bitch;
taunting you with hope
then snatching it back

– you didn't even have the courage to
face me when you told me your
insecurities had you on standby

and *why*?
why were you denying yourself of such
envied feelings?
why were you denying me of such
well-deserved euphoria?

testosterone does not fuel me
and you do not crave anything like me

and yet,
you were the one to fall first

you were the one
        to drag me down
                limb by limb
sweet-talking your way
      into my desperate heart
          only to bare your teeth
      and tear it to pieces

i should've known
      that it was destined
to expire
           maybe then,
       i wouldn't have been bruised
      so badly

ELEVATOR MUSIC

there you sit—
>a perfect ensemble of
carefully pressed skirt
>and a half moon of a smile
>>*gleaming*

like the mirror you spent
>every evening fixed to;
practising it to *perfection*

>*(how much more enjoyable*
>*this encounter would be*
>*with a little background music)*

elevator music;
>the kind of soft jazz needed
to soften such apprehensive situations

>*– an unspoken requirement*

we're too proud to admit it
though it stares us directly in the eye
>*(as we daren't)*

the thrilling awkwardness radiated from
                hesitant smiles
                        and clearing of throats;
            fidgeting with metal
makeshift weapons
            deceptive eyes fixating on
                        just about everything
                but each other

vast; all consuming
it could engulf me in an instant
and i wouldn't question it
and as time drags on and more petty
small talk is swallowed
                    i'm starting to think
                that i would embrace it.

NIHILISM

i've never been one for realism;
         my world held up
              by two opposing palms
bearing messily blended metaphors
and ever-changing answers to the
question:
               'HOW ARE YOU?'

you, on the other hand
         are all hues of reckless
            impulsive and unstoppable
in all the heights i could
         never seem to reach;
shameless in how you verbalise
every unfiltered thought
         breathing air so fresh
that each shared inhale feels like
my lungs have been
unknowingly starved 'til now

treating your lifeline
as something you can snort

it's all just some hoax—
not to be taken seriously
nor accounted for

yet, they all bounce back like rubber
hanging onto every last
facetious word that drips
from your premature lips

some sick joke, right?
and i'm your punchline
my carefully chosen inflections
are charmless next to
the irresistibility
of your spontaneity

i feel it tugging in my throat
when you are shrouded in the
admiration i fight daily for and lifted
from where i writhe;
brewing amongst
equally pathetic lovers

i suppose people
are not as they seem

i should know by now;
        we lie through our teeth
                    for validation
and receive just that;
        our thirst for acceptance
never quenched
                lying, over the years
        has become a sin
both you and i are equally
guilty of committing;
        the everlasting sourness
of our own tongues
repulsing us to the point
of flirting with the temptation
to draw azure blood
        and sink our teeth
into this bitter end

i suppose lying
is our second language;
our bond built
on a weak foundation

        and every second i feel us
            s l o w l y
falling toward our inevitable extinction.

ONE A.M.

each day of the week
is enveloped in a pained blur;
the last month a mere montage of
stomach-deep yearning

> to brush fingers;
> > lock eyes;
> > > *anything.*

infatuation is romanticised despair:
> a status that i'm silently
but proudly adorning

> the kind of unrequited romance
that reigning vultures coo over and
> grind into liquefied requirements
for addled teenagers to meet;

here,
i'll claw at my chest like an animal–
> stick my hand right through
to gift you a heart
> that no longer resides there

and if that's not enough
        i'll pry each glistening organ
one by one
from the caverns they've matured in
and parcel them up
in birthday wrapping paper

i remember it all:
every stupid anecdote;
from what jokes makes you laugh so
hard that you forget her;
to the iridescence of your features in the
sun

i'd never say a word; never out loud
and so i pool my affections
        in a notepad of lined paper
                    at one a.m.

YOU SAID THE WRONG NAME

a slip of the tongue;
a silent letter uttered aloud
nudging at your pride
                    — a precarious temper
tension bites
calls itself requited and
leaves its venomous kiss
printed into your flesh:
sanguine splattered onto
a canvas of white
                    shake yourself off.
              say it's fine.
convince them
that you don't feel it
burning through the layers of your skin
raise your brows from their knot;
a polite nod of the head
will take you further than
leaving that letter silent ever will
                    shake yourself off.
              say it doesn't matter.

– a rose by any other name
would smell just as sweet.

EGO

if you peel back my flattered flush,
there's a hidden shameful shade;
vermillion that i fight to crush
             like a debt that must be paid.

i pretend as if don't hear it
this defeating mahogany mantra
as flinching would prick up the ears
of more unseemly propaganda

i pretend as if i don't feel it
bursting through my pores
i wonder if i'd find it charming
 if it were instead seeping through yours

i pretend as if i don't taste it
this stale taste under my tongue
needing to be *needed*–
all that matters when you are young

if you peel back my bogus blush,
there's a pride that i can't gauge
something deep that thrives on the rush
             when i'm standing centre stage

LIMINAL SPACE

tears oozing from peeling duct tape;
a gratefully despondent half smile
painting me an oxymoron

> at least i didn't
> drown this time.

> at least my feet
> skimmed the cessation.

at least i didn't sell my lungs;
my eyes;
my conscience
this time and
    hopelessly depend on yours.

at least there's enough left of me
after this collision to clutch in
reconciliation
at least now the regulated, dormant
grieving can commence

> savour the burn
> this is you beginning to feel again.

THE EXACT MIDDLE

nobody asked you to draw a line
to deduce where you may stand;
yet you insist on removed neutrality
                with ruler and pen in hand

bias itself isn't inherently vulgar
but concealment contorts its shape
so as you lie sweetly through your teeth
upon your brain i scrape

each inch of the truth is veiled
in an impulse soon to be regretted
i'd rather a straightforward exile
than have falsities aided and abetted

still i pry for what lies within
for any measure of candour i can drink
but how can i expect
a grayscale painting to name me
                shades of blue or pink?

alas, you will always reside in
    the exact middle of each grievance
i know your morals are sparkling now,
but i just wanted your allegiance

NAKED

lying naked barely nudges
the level of closeness that i crave;

        claw your heart out and smudge it
            all over my lips and grave

carve into my flesh the sins that
your tongue has never tasted
and in return i'll burn the strings
attached to every chance i've wasted

for you i'll pluck my lashes;
each wish conceived with you in mind
leave marks of your love
        everywhere
          if you would be so kind

cover up your cruel facade
      and ditch me to the curb
        honey lips and soft hug eyes
and i can't express the words that are
bouncing on my tongue

SPLIT

press pause on the honeymoon;
because i'm stuck on your reaction
what you keep under lock and key
murmurs to me with endless persistence

repress the itch and crush it down
to what is deemed acceptable attraction
onlookers will recall how sweet it looked
when i slipped into co-existence

lay next to my grave
and make small talk;
   i'll try not to fixate on your tone
swear your consistency
and i'll abstain my urge to stalk
the name that most frequents your
phone

fight the need to bypass your skin;
  reprimand what burns under mine
epitomise perfection,
but you'd never win–
     not against my binary design

A CAGE OF MY OWN MAKING

heart pulsing in hand, i could never
stray too far;
i inhale

(once, twice, forever)

and there you are

button up shirt as undone as i am;
hollowed eyes a veiled threat —
                you've always been a tease.
an invitation provokes a cold sweat;
reel me in,
then release

when the day is sipped away like wine,
    and the names that slip
            from your parted lips
                    are no longer mine,

i teach myself
            to love the way
                        you trap me
from drifting
            upwards and away

THE SETTLER

growing older side by side
hopeful truths stolen by the wind

you take my hand and i sigh
        an *'is this it?'* or *'is there no end?'*

city lights and empty pockets
the thrill of change and cravings
all buried underneath the mountain
of our wedding savings

conversations and smiles are dulling
but these bars keep me from the cold
so what's another failed adventure?
at least i have a friend in growing old

counting clouds, anticipating traffic
the numbing joy in settling
masks where i'd rather be–

        fresh faces and adrenaline.

ESCAPE

i cannot recall
when the *love* was eliminated
          and the *hunt* commenced—

i suppose i couldn't pinpoint
the exact moment i realised
that you bore the cure
as well as the disease
i just synchronised
my breathing with yours
          and called it fate

they could have split
and torn my skin
shed my poisoned blood
drenched me in it
and remain oblivious still i would
night by night, asleep
in the hurricane of your embrace
not once do i consider taking shelter

we cave into our abdomens;
into the very pit of our souls
to hide from the fierce reign of change
the toxicity of the air we breathe
matters not
when we have grown overfamiliar
with the sting
now we beg the infected needle
to pierce our tortured skin
                    (we don't know any better)

i suppose that to some extent,
we are both to blame
        myself, a part-time masochist
for chasing my own agony
            and *you*, dearest dealer
for gratifying my addiction
supplying the most
haunting highs and lows
i've ever felt

it is in situations like this
where the lines blur for me
and i cannot make sense
of who is the true villain:
                    the torturer?
                    or the enabler?

ii.

winter

A FRESH START

let the picture perfect children decay
                      rot like aged fruit cores;
neatly and precisely parcelled up
then tucked away
at the very bottom
        of your never ending desk drawer

spilling your guts
only leads to a barren stomach;
            a wasteland where
butterflies used to crowd
now, not a single thread
of conscience is left
to press you to watch
the insufferable memories burn;
to laugh light-heartedly and let
goodbyes after goodbyes tumble
incessantly from your lips
to relieve your aching mind
and divorce the past

but temptation burns
    oh, what i wouldn't give to relive
        that juvenile fantasy once more!

HERE'S WHAT I REMEMBER

endless noise
                    and blinding lights

the glow of your eyes
                              fizzling out
                    into the night

each of your vocal inflections;
                    every hiss and every rasp

my rhythmic porn star moans;
                              chest hollowing
                    out *more*
with each gasp

i remember fighting until dawn
                    too exhausted to make up;

mementoes of
                    stress
                              and
                              joy

                    that i learned to cover up

i remember when you came home
      wrapped up in the scent of
            someone else's perfume

i remember the way
      you'd hold me tight
        on a brisk winter's afternoon

i remember every sunrise
      and each sunset

but if i'm being honest,

i'd rather forget.

AFTERGLOW

draw the curtains, love
      they don't need to see this part.

the peeling of
      lifeless bodies
from where they
      s t i c k
         like wet cement

onto windows,
      pavements,
         the walls
  of the master bedroom.

the merciless drowning
     of the carpet
in sickly sweet lavender;

masking the shameful stains
    left by abused substances
       and one night stands alike

there's a reason why
        we don't talk about
                the morning after.

the fuzzy, overexposed hours
        of rejecting the thinned linings
of your stomach,
        only to mourn them
                in aching silence

denting the wall
with your temple;
        your foot;
                your nails

desperate trials
        to eradicate all memory
                of your one night wonder

WHEN THE GLASS SHATTERED

your averted eyes
             and charismatic prowl;
masterfully smoothing over
             excuse
                   after excuse

my lips, you kiss
             but my heart, you befoul

if i hadn't clung so desperately,
             i could have questioned
your motives from the start
                   but alas, you knotted me
             around your finger
had me convinced i had infiltrated
                   that blackened heart

me, donning my inexperience and
       cupping my fragility - heart in hand

claiming you merely 'took advantage'
is too honey-sweet an accusation
                   not after each cover story
             you meticulously planned

it was on those sleepless nights
when i finally caught up to the truth

i could no longer deny
the subtext of secrecy
or ascribe it to the horrors
of your youth

maybe it wasn't you
i believed too strongly in;
maybe it was the hope
that the worst was over
that i had faced my fiercest battles
and never again would i fight for closure

that explains each dismissed glance at
another;
each all-consuming jealous phase and
every mark of strange behaviour

maybe in the end,
it wasn't you i was excusing,
            it was me i was protecting.

CONTEMPLATIONS OF A BROKEN MIND

i have always imagined that
if you burrow deep enough inside
yourself;
                              wrap yourself around
that pulsating organ
                       that keeps you alive;

familiarise yourself first-hand
with the mechanisms responsible for
your survival;

you'd encounter
                  - a control panel -
displaying all available
          emotional responses;

each gleaming button wired
          to a different abundance of
chemicals to release–

               where you could methodically
          filter emotions in and out

where you can shut off the desperation;
                    the aching loneliness
            in a bustling crowd;

the moving-towards-nothing-
but-away-from-everything

for good

                        if you wanted to

a way of asserting control
            at times when i am dethroned by
my emotional sensitivity

            or rather a harrowing reminder
that we have all degraded ourselves
            into nothing more than machines

sometimes i dream about
finding myself buried
                side by side with
each causality
of my decayed relations;
                each misstep
                        and shadowed regret

and when i wake,
i interrogate myself
to breaking point
before slumping in defeat
and assigning my
                    not-so perfect childhood
as the culprit
            to my not-so conceptual suicide

even after shattering the glass
that separates myself from my demons
        i still can not locate exactly
                    where it all went wrong;
too fearful to insult the sensations
that have dominated me
and yet i actively seek the same
watered down,
condescending comments

that have been echoed
            a million times before
for some kind
            of consistency in my life

THAT NIGHT IN THE WOODS

would you allow me
        to rinse you down?

washing away the *panic*
        that you just can't seem
                to shudder off

paranoia waits to pounce
        around every last
                corner you turn
in your feeble
        attempts to escape

                but you're too late

each cut-throat remark has
snaked its way
        around the cogs in your head
and ensnared your will to fight back

would you allow me to shred
        the abundance of dead leaves
that you choke on
from the moment you wake

to free you properly from
        that night in the woods

too arduous a task; your garden
            is brimming with empty graves
from your attempts
    to bury the hatchet
            and move on

                        but the scent
                        of the damp
                        is still lodged
                        inside your nostrils

the winding, curled arms of the trees
flex towards you in a perverted embrace

would you allow me
        to tear away each branch?
seize the power to
deliver retribution

healing isn't linear
not when the past still finds a way
to slit your hopes

to bring you right back to
                your roots

                                those roots
to bring you back
                to every raised brow
                                from mislabelled enablers
to every cruel name now tattooed under
your skin and embedded in your
nightmares

to every cry that ripped
                from your throat
                                that night in the woods

would you allow me
                rinse you down?

to map constellations
                in the water
                                so that you can
lay amongst the stars
                far away from here.

CHEATERCHEATERCHEATER

you feel like a bullet
        training in on my abdomen
penetrating the thin layers of flesh,
      and tearing my resilience like mesh

a seemingly constant barreling
into the depths of my skull–
        crushing my perceptions
                and reactions

rendering me brain-dead
until it feels like every joint
that constructs me
is instead constructed
of lead

you feel like death,
        stone-cold death
             to-be-feared death

tear-me-up-and-stuff-me-
*down-the-drain-*death

inching along my flesh
            and pulling the plug
washing away my ability to say:

                              'NO!'
                              'STOP!'

it was never the same after that:
    silent mornings
    absent evenings
    avoided glances
    stiffened dances
        and a surging sense of loneliness
                              on my behalf

your sweet apple cider
        is now bland and tasteless, my dear
faded, along with those
                once romanticised memories

                    i fear,
                        will we ever learn
                        to shrink back inside
                            of ourselves?
doting upon each other;
        veiled by fabricated masks
of people we used to know

and still, after days of
        roaming around my gut
in search of some kind of change
some kind of proof we were estranged,
        i crawl back

internal organs stuffed into my pockets
staining my perfectly pressed
swing dress scarlet
        i crawl b a c k

thinking if i repaint the walls mahogany
your affair will no longer
bother me

        *i crawl **back***

        empty.

BODY

the price i'll pay
for selling myself to the operating table;

hips the width of my throat
                              lips trembling
           a pathetic mantra of
                           "i'm ready."
head lifted too high to
             cast a glance down
at what's crumbling
              where i stand

                        and so i walk
              into the burning building
          i once called home
          — i can't trust myself anymore.

the price i'll pay for
familiarising myself with weaponry;
a scalpel
      becoming my closest friend
in how it teasingly slices;
        peels off the layers of my skin
i'm not too fond of;

the parts of myself
                i could do without
until enough is enough
                and i don't even recognise
                        myself anymore.

but how do you tell when it's too much?

extremists have always
                bared their teeth and
                        they've never offered
                a helping hand
to people like me
                with conflicting thoughts
                        and childish brains.

WHAT YOU LEFT OF ME

place me beneath your microscope;
                there's sensuality
in the way you examine,
        slice and inspect my temporal lobe;
such erotica begs you to come in

open up my chest cavity;
find the core of my disruptions

            though flip the switch and
you'll find apathy
            unswayed by the most
                    compelling seductions

piece by piece
        take a closer look
            at the mangled corpse
                    that loved you

flip my pages
                like a book
and sniff
            my growing stench
                        like glue

MY LAMP

this lamp
      feels like confined sunlight

the unyielding heat
          when i press close
feels like when you would
          spill laughter upon my cheek
in all its breathy, goosebump-y glory

my brain rattles melodically
against the confinements of my skull

i hear it quiver with every silence;
          every gap you used to fill
but with my lamp,
          my mind is sedated
and i can recount
          all our shared summers
      and the radiance of your smile

this lamp promises me
forever
its leash ensuring me
that it could never stray far

i feel i may never begin to miss you
        when you stay trapped
                within this glass

the nights are the hardest,
but my lamp provides the warmth
        you took when you departed

i think if i stare hard enough
it'll reveal your fingerprints
still branded on its switch

recall when we bought this lamp;
our first piece of shared furniture
a symbol of our promised future
           but now you're gone and

inside,
i am e m p t y
        so empty
      emptyemptyemptyempty

except for
this lamp.

INTIMACY

my skin is no longer mine; it seems
        pinching my arm feels like
every covert tug in public
that served as
a subliminal warning for
private repercussions
i'd anxiously await

i dry myself down
        with the towel that dried you

        finding sanctuary in intimacy that
i am in the driver's seat for

you crushed my voice box
        and in its place instilled
                a ticking time bomb

                    over my eyes,
        you stuck a greyscale filter
and so i passed by every red flag

like a fool, i am now sentenced
to haunting nightmares and
a broken record looping your commands

closing my eyes only reveals yours;
            and through yours
                i see the pieces of myself
            that you left behind;
fathomless
                drained of colour
and purpose.

you are the bad thing
    that even pessimists cannot stand—
        pushed to *finally* engulf themselves
in the sickeningly eagerly flames
that lash around now
        in the barren chasm of my stomach

i still have yet to comprehend
the dripping dread
on its way to
swallow me whole
                (only i am blatantly lying,
                because i know exactly
                why i am empty)

yet i cling
to this illusion
like a sickeningly thin lifeline
and cover my ears
when you try to shatter them
with imperatives

my pulse beats
    like a caged butterfly
        against the beds of your
          dagger-like fingers
     when you are pressing them
      deep
into the thinness of my wrists;
     flesh soaking up
    every last filthy word
   you can muster the courage
      to think of;
secured
around my trachea,
crushing everything
i'm trying to scream at you

i suppose
that is one way
to shut me up—
        to mercilessly assault my mind
     rid it of all conventional thoughts
and stuff it full of your own
                 (at least then
                 we'll have something
                    in common)

i am ducking my head
under the tsunami
along with yours
        because even now,
i am p e t r i f i e d
    of being singled out.

      i do not crave the lingering guilt
    that comes with being labelled
        the only survivor on deck.

it is the way you speak those
forbidden words
so nonchalantly that
challenges my sanity
         not each slash to my
      already broken mind,

i am used to the surprises by now
and you have given up
on attempting to catch me off-guard.

and that's just it, isn't it?
                  because i am never off-guard,
i have eyes ripping through my skull
just to keep tabs on you.

no, it is your words
that tear me up inside
how you cause me to feel stripped
raw and bleeding
                        when i am fully
            clothed and breathing

with just three words

and even after how you devour
                        any remainder of joy
juxtaposed with my sour mindset,

i am on my knees pleading,
begging for *more*
                  and *more*
                              *and **more***

because at least you aren't
neglecting me any longer.

my face:
        tear stricken
and vulnerable

my body:
        a massacre
of blended blood
and regret

                        why do i not stop you?
you are killing me,
        and i am *allowing* you

you paint violet bruises
onto the too-forgiving canvas
of my exposed skin
and i call it *art*;

you will
    yank my organs out
                one by one,
                    uttering the words

        'i know what i'm doing'

you

destroyed

my mind

and with my mind,

e v e r y t h i n g

came tumbling down.

iii.

spring

WE KILLED THE PLANET

the end is near;
both our consensus and mantra

birthed from
wistful, icy memories
            toxified (by us)
into no more than
a crumbling foundation

            there is nothing left for us here

it's like every apocalyptic movie:
the bad thing infiltrates
every corner
of every room
and the saviour complexes
step up to restore our ignorance

                    but there's no bliss in what is
                            irreversible;
                    when *we* made the bad thing

i think in the end,

    i'll savour my last moments
        alone

acknowledging my own reflection
in my tv screen;

eyes glinting

    with fear,

        and nails bitten

           to the core

the optimists among us
claim the end is but a benchmark:
                              a fresh start

killers swept up
          by extraterrestrials
coded all too forgiving
                    in my binary morality
and humanity will be repurposed

 everything happens for a reason, right?

maybe it's selfish
to think of this
as the end

maybe the extraterrestrials
have been
eagerly watching
our self-destruction
all along;

eyes glinting

                    in the reflections
                              of their screens

WHEN I OPENED MY EYES

i watched an actor's final curtain call;

THE ROLE: a melodramatic satire
of the person i had once so
apologetically adored;

THE ACTOR: less charming counterpart
now so vividly coloured all shades of
ruthless and vile

and i suppose if i had ever truly
found solace in your parody,
   i would've hardly recognised you at all

i used to boast about my 20/20 vision
praising my biology for where it excelled
as a way of shrouding the more

                    UNSPEAKABLE PARTS:
my orientations deemed unnatural; and
my disproportionate abundance of
chemicals; my palpitations that lack
causality; and the sponge like texture of
my heart.

but now i see you for the very first time
and i realise that even my most
remarkable qualities
ironically mirror your own dishonesty
(am i delusional enough
to have ignored
that we have been on stage
this entire time?)

take your final bow now,
as contemplation
only ignites resentment over

SO MANY years wasted
SO MANY sunlit evenings missed
enduring the unendurable

deep within my belly
behind my engulfing resentment
growls the lasting effects of your cruelty

imposter syndrome lingers
and batters my worth;
was it my fault for not seeing the signs?
should i berate myself for being so blind?

but it was still you
when i opened my eyes:

flaccid,
erratic
and embarrassingly *real*

and it had always been you
to my greatest surprise

SEPARATION

the initial split; the pinnacle of change
masked by fear of the unknown
swayed by manipulations
over the phone;
speak up
or join the firing range

the thrill of this twisted debate
        is eager to yank you
                in one direction
           life-changing decisions
        rooted in inflection
and perks that soon stagnate

relate each shirk and wound alike
to some unexplainable depression
independence ignites regression
        to tearing stabilisers
                from your bike

you'd think i'd be rehearsed
this loss draining me
                    not once, but twice
but after soaking
in empty advice
and labelling myself
'cursed' –

i rearrange my pulled-apart limbs
            and construct myself
                        a pair of wings

NYMPHO

you reek of desperation;
                              offering up the body
              we repurposed together
to people with pretty eyes
                    and prettier smiles

you keep these people
              (pretty people with skin
                        that you yearn to taste)
stowed away in the
              drawer under your bed,
                              sleeping soundly
              among the birthday cards
from your deadbeat dad
                    'out of sight and out of of mind'
as they say

you pine incessantly
like an insufferable toddler
for what you just *couldn't*
              accept from me

i wonder how many have traced
    the answers *i* printed into your chest.
ricochetting your guilt and
ensuring it sinks
deep into my gut

you allowed me to laugh at the jokes
of the people you screwed
behind closed doors.

                          did i really lower
                             your standards
                                that much?

was it the evenings you felt
        compelled to hold my frame
                    as it raked with sobs?

    or maybe the nights you spent
clothed in the thickest of tension;
        sat shaking in the hospital car park?

            did my mania
    make me less fuckable to you?

funny, because
i thought you liked damage.

filter me out
and invite in the new;
                    did you even mourn?
or did you dust me
from the crevices of your heart
as swiftly as you invited them in?
                    is there even a heart left
in that cool pillow
        i used to rise from each morning?

you smile the same smile

                and i feel like
                        d y i n g

carelessly collect me up
then let me fall
at the sight of someone
newer and *shinier*;
not yet rusting from
your manipulation.

you laugh and you're '*doing well*';
and i don't think i ever
really knew you

now you have the nerve
to play the part of the wounded soldier
    when you're still holding the bayonet

the best part is
you're aware of your own
tarred morality

          — why else would you keep them
            shrouded in lies and deceit?

your guilty conscience
    will be your undoing

the bile in my throat is for you
    and as i spit it over
where we lay, i'll vow
    to finally stop
        tearing myself apart.

CLOSURE

candle wax drips just
ahead of my heartbeat
and moulds
with your carpet
              —cementing that you could
              never scrub me away completely

    we are a renaissance painting
        of a virtual screen
YOU: the most gorgeous nightmare,
and
ME: stuck rewriting my soliloquies
            —constantly rescaling myself
               for your satisfaction

healing presents itself in
Drunken Confessions
and Transferred Affections
it births hopes that
Maybe
one day the itch
in my head will cease
when my phone exposes your location
at
an address i don't recognise

i'd hunt and hoard
your premature teeth in a jar
just to treasure one part of **You**
that could never abandon me like this

what ever happened to the infatuated
children?
why are we standing here,
teeth bared,
in their places?

we are forcibly performing roles
that we have long outgrown
   —did we keep our lips buttoned out of
    prideful shame or lingering respect?

the alarm clock
rattling my skull is shrieking and
it's **You**
i burn and break for

i beg to comprehend
any language
but yours—
to breathe
and move
freely

having exited your chess game for good;
a stalemate has never before
served as such a blessing

i would deflower your grave
before embracing it,
a satirical subversion
                with the sole intent
                        of final closure.

EPILOGUE

your infiltration demands gratitude
       and most often i will acquiesce

tentatively, i'll invite you
down my throat
and seek solace in a covert mantra—
that one day
the bruises you inflict will blur
into nothing more than a bad dream

with empty promises
and romantic deceit,
you keep me forcibly pinned
to our timeline
and i thank you with
all the compliments
i should reserve for my
meditation podcast.

weighted arms arch around me
and cage my insecurities;
perhaps if you squeeze hard enough,
you'll melt my doubts too?

drinking you in tastes like
the medicine i was ordered
to take as a child
and i want nothing more than to
                              spit you out
but you mould a house
                    out of my sighs
and i convince myself
                    that it is my
                              forever home

returning to a pixelated portrait
              of you and i will never
be harder to resist
                    not now that my tongue
is still tingling with you on my lips;
                    not now that my fingers
are still searing with yearning
              from your last magical touch
as i fall once more,
my rationality implores me to catch
myself
              (it knows you won't do it for me)
and in utter desperation,
i rattle my skull and
scream until my throat is
red and *raw*;

it's in my best interests
to accessorise you with
caution tape
and crimson paint
until i can finally take a hint.

cold bites at each exposed
fragment of flesh,
serving as a cool and deflating reminder
               that i'm alive, still
i find that there is more than you
 and the confinements
of my four walls

everything and nothing
douses the memories i have of you
and i feel i am *drowning* in your absence

for evermore
i will resemble a tortured artist
with you as
my eternal muse:

                    shall i paint you
                    as a saint today,
                    or the villain
                    who stole
                    my innocence?

now, i resent you
                  that much is clear

i resent you for keeping me
neatly packaged out of the way
                  (complete with
                  exhaustive nights
                  of gaslighting
                  and a pretty bow on top)

i resent you for hindering my growth;
for the intrusion you left
within my adolescent mind

i resent you for discarding me
the moment loving me was no longer
convenient for you

some days
i'm sure that i'll outgrow you for good;
memories and pain intact

others i wake gasping for air,
certain that i can still feel
the threatening pads of your fingers
                  pressed into my throat.

days are growing shorter;
                        darker
but within this, i find comfort
i fell for you in broad daylight

                                        so
the night is what heals me now

i tease the soles of my shoes
            with late night strolls
and teach my throat to scream
            the lyrics of my favourite songs
instead of pleas for you to stay

you, i leave behind
            with all my burnt wax
                        and cried tears
as i abandon the fragile shell
of who i was and
            piece myself
                        back together.

VIRGINITY

virginity is a construct
drawn directly from the dicks
of brainless boys
thirsty for purer pussy;
branding female counterparts
whorish to distract
from their own desperate lust for
a clumsy stroking of their ego

virginity is a lie
whispered to make girls feel unclean
for spreading their legs
whilst men gain
another sparkling badge
on their sleeve

it's a farce
used to demean:
there's nothing liberating
about damaged goods

virginity is unfair
ascribing every girl mary or eve
before she even sees sixteen;
the weight of the word is enough
to collapse starving girls
who stay home sick from school
                           and can't face
            the shower anymore

virginity is a weapon
used to slaughter unafraid lambs
drilling misogynistic narratives
into every underdeveloped brain—

                  'nobody will love you
                  if you aren't fully theirs;
                        love is supposed
                  to make your heart drop'

relish being
      his most prized possession
                           to sit pretty on
his mantelpiece

for him to boast about and
                           for his clan to
defame

without consequence
                                    over a pint

but how ever can he achieve that
                    if your body isn't up for sale?

it's every little girl's dream
                    to grow up to do what she's told

virginity is a construct
                    because if not,
it was stolen from me

instead of a night under the stars,
                    i got jabs at bathing suit parts

UNREQUITED

with each vaguely concealed smirk
and every careful
unfolding of vulnerability,
the gap between us feels
progressively metaphysical;
foolish
my eyes are so trained on you
that i forget to acknowledge
the pane of glass separating us

i wonder if you'll ever honour me
    with satisfying these delusions,
       or perhaps crush them into dust?

i both crave and fear your verdict;
        will you allow me to indulge
      in limbo for one moment longer?

but at the same time
that i dance with temptation;
every second i spend anticipating a
brush of fingers;
or locking of eyes
burns more fiercely
than the coffee pot we both reached for

i'm slowly,
painfully
dying;

        will i be the embarrassing story
           that you tell at christmas?
laughing away
unrelenting, childish love

  or will you spend those winter nights
        huddled by the fire?
wishing it was *my warmth* blanketing
you

i worry that when you leave for good
        you'll leave behind a gap
i can't help
but acknowledge

your absence
will send me into spirals of
        '*what if*'s
          and regret
and i'll be cast out
of the confined space
we found solace in

you render me mad and
i need you
to clarify for me:
        is this real?

we are a million worlds away;
both on the cusp
of new adventures
        that don't even slightly align

so *why*
            am i still so fixated on you?

why
               does your aftershave
                 call my name?

DAY IN THE LIFE

to open my eyes to a kinder world—
        heart never knowing the panic
of taking up too much space;
                knuckles never feeling
the cool metal of my keys
                  when i walk home

privilege presents itself before you
in a stairway;
anything's attainable with
        enough charm and cock
                    i suppose

if you took my place
        would you be scared?
would you hastily
        yank down your skirt
                each time you caught
        a whiff of testosterone?
would you be *ashamed*
        of the body you inhabit
for the way
        it opens you up to onslaught?
as if there were a target painted
in the centre of your chest

to hold the power
you've always abused
in my little finger
would be unseemly
(we both know it
but only one
seems to mind)

    watch that apathy transcribe to rage
          at four simple syllables;

my mere existence fetishised
and you expect me to take pity
          on your self-fulfilling prophecy

FEVER DREAM

you wore my skin
inside out
dangled polaroids of my organs
from fairy lights

       oh, back then i was *everywhere*

we exchanged each other's breaths
and now by default,
my lungs work twice as hard

       i suppose that you just
       left so quickly
       i catch myself wondering
       if you were but a fever dream

i'm two steps behind again;
blanketed in
       mortification and *betrayal*

i wake each day to a mantra of
       'but it's better now'
and i suppose it's better
       to be alone
       than to feel lonely

tell me,
how easily was it
        to cut me out?
photoshop doesn't work on guilty minds
but you can always try to conceal the
past

        do you ever miss me back?
    do you think about all we went though?

limbo feels like
wading into the deepest sea
play time is over
yet all fingers are pointed at me

and truly, i'll be okay
     i ride the bus alone each day
and *really* i'm over it;
        it only hurts a bit
                or at least
that's what i can stomach to say

VIRGINITY (REVISITED)

fingers that caress,
                 not scratch
and tears that express
            and narrow the gap
or recognise my own and match
            not guilt-trip or prelude a snap

hesitation and requests
in place of forced entry

     and now i barely even notice the ceiling

each nudge and touch
given gently
sends my body into
gyrations of healing

movements synchronised
            and gasps harmonised;

in affection that's authorised,
       we find intimacy revised

REBIRTH

i get off at a different bus stop now;
i still see you waiting for me
at the old one,
> *perfectly painted smile intact*

you are the thing
buried within me
that i wanted to kill—
> the reason i can't help
> but check over my
> shoulder when crossing
the same streets i used to cross with
you;
forevermore tainted
> by your web of lies and illusions

i don't think i'll stop ever being angry at
you;
angry at how deeply i bled
angry that you still don't even
acknowledge that *you* were the one
wielding the knife

you make your appearances
          in claustrophobic flashbacks
where i feel my dirtiest
          and nightmares
                where i never escaped you

the realisation that i unpeeled my heart
          for a stranger cuts deeper than
your cruellest words

  i wish you no longer crossed my mind

that i could dance down the street
                on my way to the bus stop

i wish my subconscious could
bar you from entry
that your sickening smile
never flicks behind my eyes again

so i get off at a different bus stop
                walk down different paths
and i hope
that one day
          those old streets
                              (and i)
          will feel new again.

MY FESTERING NEED TO BE GOOD

in your absence,
        i compartmentalise
           my nine o'clock appetites

URGES:
to desperately shave off layers of pink
flesh
to further mutilate and criminalise
myself
to fill the void with whatever i can,
sweet or savoury

to avoid slurring my guilt
      in the interrogative morning light

watch as it tickles
      my now lavender cheek
          weary and wilted

after a night of compacted
manifestations

my greatest accomplishment?
perfecting my easy-on-the-tongue,
seamlessly congruent facade

the type of person your parents could
love;
                              the ideal candidate

unproblematically boring;
                    sweetly empty and endearing

in how her eyes roll to the back of her
rattling skull

on evenings i soak
                 in shades of greyscale
to reinforce my subdued categorisation

                    whilst the thrashing violence
                         remains neatly confined
           underneath my button up shirt

press play and like clockwork,
i'll lifelessly emerge at an imperfect
hour
i'll eat three meals a day and get
straight As

the scars that once littered my skin
        have now been sealed under paint
and i can enter a room without sinking
beneath the floorboards

                                alas, again
            my countenance will betray me

what i tried to bury
will squeeze me to a pulp
and again
the vehement truth spills
like every last morsel i forced
down my throat
every lie i told my mother and
every promise to change

            *i'll always end up disappointing
                    the people i love.*

THE SUN (i)

a gentle grip around my heart
        and contagious smiles;
you love me the way
that children love recess and dress up
and i look at you
with all of the unbridled giddiness
i used to feel the night
before my birthday

you teach me what hope feels like
and it's *you*;
it's early morning kisses that
nourish me for the whole day;
it's that very first grin and
the very last wave;
it's the chime of your laugh and
the blue in your eyes

i keep expecting to sober up;
to open my eyes and mourn this
beautiful, impossible dream
but you're not slipping away and
        is this acceptance?

my inhibitions melt with the sun's rays
and suddenly,
          i'm reborn again

i cradle you with the same care and
intensity my mother did unto my eldest
sister

i hope that i learn from her mistakes;
that i won't press you too close that you
resent me;
that the glasses we adorn are unbiased;
and that your tongue, delivering only
truths and satisfactions, will keep me
afloat for the foreseeable

i ask myself:
          'do i deserve this?'
when you press dangerously close
          to peeling back my ugliest layers

'i think i must'
          as you drift asleep
                    but never away
comfortably cradled by me,
          damage and all intact

painstakingly
with my finger and thumb,
i can trace the cracks in your heart
it's true, you've also
been broken before

we're too familiar
with the artistry of
glueing ourselves back together
but never before
blanketed in the safety
of solidarity

i love you with every wrong turn and
every fumble; with each pause and
crescendo
i love you with every wish for greener
grass and puff of cold air
on that first night
in rekindled company

the charred parts of myself
fearlessly blossom in your presence
and whilst you couldn't fix me
and i would not mend you
sunlight is inviting and coaxes the
moon from its cavern

your matured eyes bare the same
liveliness as before
albeit worn by experience and tears
shed;
i hope mine glisten
with all the warmth i feel within
whenever we sit
            perfectly entangled
                on those glowing evenings
                    and quiet mornings

YOUR GENETIC GIFT

i didn't notice it at first —
the way that your evening glass of wine
alone, could no longer
quench your thirst;
                         ignited dependence
                           highlighted your
                                  decline

i didn't notice
until it consumed me too —
             until my only friend was
                        a demeaning blade;
glinting with temptations that only
grew; atoning me for each moral debt i
paid

demonised in the wide screen
                but for us, it was our lifeline

before the medicine
             became the disease
when we lied
            and convinced them
we were *fine*

i hope to earn the forgiveness
                of those i once deceived
though you could beg forever
                and never receive mine

without you, i stand proud
at ten months clean

and hope that one day
                i'll be able to stand red wine.

ELLIPSIS

our history stylised
    like the movies you don't understand
our summer-long emails prized;
our   knuckle-biting   chess   games
unplanned

skip to fantasising about domesticity
        then a crescendo under the moon
still mending from bone-deep toxicity
        but i don't think that it's too soon

hot chocolates and nervous laughter;
then your warmth softening my terrors
a   resolution   we   didn't   have   to   chase
after;
we   fell   into   place   after   fumbles   and
errors

lips rekindled and stability
        in our silent conversations
bears witness to that
        first clumsy touch
requited   love   never   swayed   by
temptations
consoles the fear of loving too much

THE SUN (ii)

i've spent my life seeking subtext
so forgive me for overthinking a phrase,
my unprompted outbursts leave you
perplexed;

>> words heated enough
>> to ignite a blaze

but with swollen lips
>> and exchanged tears,
>> i trust you more than i trust road signs

you renew my worth;
>> wash away my shameful fears;
>> your feet freely bound by vines
to the same solid earth
>> i can't help but tread with haste,
though i've walked this route a million
times—

>> my mind stuck on:
>>> debating my worth;
>>> losing your taste;
>>> and the paranoia of
>>> repeated past crimes

with each unforgiving jolt at your touch,
it presses closer
                and suddenly i'm too much

i replay our winter evening drives
when, in between snapshots
                       of your profile
and eyes like waves tickling the shore,
we'd profess our love through the
prosaic guise of rhymes, couplets and
freestyle; howling in unison 'til our
throats were sore

if you only knew the trance
that you have me under;
             inner child cradled
                  in your scarred hands

only to your love would i surrender
the incoherent confessions
      that no other soul could understand

to you, my truth is another dialect
and i've gorged each page of your
prelude;
although your phrasing remains
imperfect
and over former lovers, my guilty party
broods—

    my heart expands night and day
    to accommodate all i feel for you

and whilst on the chance falter we may,
i   defy   chance
and strive
        to see this through.

AN UNBURIABLE HATCHET

i can still feel you
sometimes
            in a sharp flicker of a moment
right before i catch myself;
when i choke on the sour taste of
conversation;
when i can foretell an abrupt exit
            after every intrusion;
                        and every hot tear

the pebbles you toss
            at my window
are starting to ricochet
                        once or twice
                  i'll let my guard down
as you coerce me
            into letting in
some *sweet summer air*

and sometimes you'll hurt me still
                  your pebbles will fatten
            into monstrous rocks
as they're advancing

strike me
       once,
            twice

               but *fail* to crush me down
          to where i started

i'll greet you as an old friend;
but never embrace you as a lover

despite the fact
       you never fail
          to make my heart

              skip

                    a
                         beat.

Printed in Great Britain
by Amazon

25023513R00067